Little book,
BIG truth!

Tina M. Levene

ISBN-13: 978-1511453929

Dedication

This book is dedicated to you!

To all of the young people I have met and to those of you that I am yet to meet one day. This is for the young ones that have gone on to be successful and those that have died. As an adult that teaches, listens to and learns from youth, it is not only my profession but my passion. Notice I said, 'listens to'?

As an adult, it is my job to actually listen to you. I care about you and want to know what you are thinking, feeling and doing. I want to know what your dreams are and what your fears consist of.

This book is dedicated to young people because you are our 'now', not just our future. You are not a mistake. You are worthy of love. You have a purpose and you can make a difference in this world. Let's start with you.

Little book, BIG truth!

Foreword

Don't be fooled by Tina's relentlessly cheerful and electrifying energy. This is a woman whose grace is borne of her suffering and struggle.

Little book, BIG truth! is Tina's latest publication that chooses to live in the solution - not the problem.

Practical and plainspoken, we are taken on a journey in search of our authentic selves.

Tina is the quintessential big sister, offering at once sage counsel, and that most precious of elements - real hope.

Raynard Dean Packard

Director, The Packard Institute, Inc.

Little book, BIG truth!

THANK YOU!

Thank you! I appreciate that you chose this book to read. Your time, energy and investment in you are very important to me. I am grateful you have the desire to find out what the BIG T.R.U.T.H. is!

First and foremost, be grateful this is not in my handwriting and it is typed! Secondly, this book is considered 'little' because if you are anything like me, you are busy and do not have time for long books. Oh yeah, and also I have ADHD. LOOK SQUIRREL! Thirdly, we have a lot in common; I was once your age. I know, hard to believe, right? So, why did I write a book for young people like you?

The truth is that for over 17 years, I have worked with young people. Special, young people just like you. Young people that have big dreams. Young people that have lost all of their hope. Young people that have been victimized by violence and had encountered horrible experiences. Youth that have not had the best of role models in their lives. Young people that feel pressured everyday to be perfect. Young people that wish they had never been born. Young people that cannot see passed their pain.

Can you relate? Maybe you have felt pressured to be perfect or pressure to pass that big test? Or you have so much pain inside you; you are looking to let it escape quickly to relieve the hurt?

I am not only an advocate for young people, I absolutely LOVE young people! You are so creative, intelligent, fun and straight up…cool.

Throughout this book, I hope you get a 'little' hope, a 'little' inspiration and a 'little' motivation through my crazy, close to death experiences. Don't be afraid…I am not saying you need to be perfect in this book! None of us are, so do not worry. No, I do not want you to be like someone else! And you certainly are not an alien!

Just be…YOU!!!!

I'm just saying!

My request right now is that you will have an open mind while reading this little book.

This is where you yell: 'What? Open my mind? What does that even mean, Tina?' Okay, simmer down tiger!

Here is an example; can you add 2 numbers together to equal the number 9? $5 + 4 = 9$ Right?

But, did everyone come up with those exact two numbers to equal the number 9? Probably not.

Who came up with $8 + 1 = 9$? Raise your hand…I cannot hear you! LOL

What about $6 + 3 = 9$?

Anyone think of $7 + 2 = 9$?

Do not worry, this is the only Math you will be required to endure throughout this whole 'little' book. Wipe the sweat off your perfect eye brow and chill out.

Part of having an open mind is 'thinking outside of the box'. Do I mean an actual cardboard box? Like a big refrigerator box that was the best toy ever when you were a little kid? No, I mean instead of thinking $5 + 4 = 9$ is the only RIGHT way to equal 9 is not having an open mind. As indicated above, we found other numbers to equal 9. Look at the big picture; always ask yourselves "Is there more to this situation or problem?"

How does this apply to my life Tina? I am so glad you asked me.

Why is having an open mind important for a young person?

As a young person, I hope you can understand that everyone has a story. Not everyone grew up like you. Not everyone thinks like you and not everyone will like you. This is the truth in everyone's life, especially throughout your life the older you get. If you learn this now, you will save yourself a ton of heart ache! Just have an open mind and listen to others, it does not mean you have to agree with them 100% of the time.

Do you know how much time people lose by trying to convince other people to like them? Seriously, think about it. Did you ever change your opinion about something just because someone you wanted as a friend thought differently than you? Have you ever changed your hair, maybe got a new cut or color, because someone told you it should look different? Did you get a permanent scar or tattoo just because someone told you to do something?

The truth is that most people are control freaks and try to 'control' you or gain power over you because it gives them a sense of superiority. If they cannot control themselves, they want to try to control others including you.

I learned this at an early age. I thought to myself, *If I do what others suggested, who cares what I want to do.* Where did that thinking get me? I hated myself for it. I dismissed my feelings and valued others opinions more than my own. I was miserable; never happy and felt like I could never please anyone.

Stop people pleasing!

I remember trying to please everyone around me and who suffered the most? Me!

So, back to having an open mind, are you still with me? HELLO?

You will learn things in this book that will help you throughout your whole life. Is it hard to imagine you will most likely live another 60-70 years? Well, if you eat healthy, take care of your brain, heart and lungs; you have a chance to live longer than your great grandparents. Cool huh?

LOL

(Read in your most dramatic voice.)

The stage was set. The audience was in place, waiting patiently for my big entrance. I could feel the warmth of the spot light upon my face as I walked out onto the platform to perform the funniest of all my sketches. The host announced me as the next contestant to *WOW* the audience. My mission was to create the biggest, best abruption of laughter ever known to this TV show, "MAKE ME LAUGH." As I took my position at center stage, I gave a small glance into the huge arena filled with audience members and their eager chants to 'make me laugh' began.

"Make me laugh! Make me laugh!"

Silence deafened my ears as I felt the spot light burn the top of my head. I peered down, focused on the stage floor and fell to my knees.

Remember when I said about 'Stop People Pleasing?' At this moment in my young three year old life, I had a choice.

#1 Continue to use all of my energy to 'make the audience laugh'

OR

#2 Use that energy to just have fun and forget about what others thought of me.

I chose #1; I fell to my knees and walked over to the front door. As I was making funny noises and faces, the audience began to expel murmurs of breath as if they were holding back, with all their might, loads of laughter. With one look to the audience, I swiftly raised my left arm, clinched my left hand into a fist and pierced my hand straight through...the glass window!

Needless to say, no one laughed, no one murmured a word except my older sister who screamed at the top of her lungs! As soon as the 'audience', which consisted of just 6-7 childhood friends/neighbors sitting on my living room couch, realized I had indeed busted my hand and arm through a glass window in the front door. Not one friend laughed, in fact, they actually ran home screaming and crying.

Blood squirted up and out and all around. Looked like a sprinkler at the water park! I remember grabbing my arm and looking at it. I was centimeters away from severing my main artery in my left wrist.

To make a long story short, what began as a fun day inside playing with friends and trying to make them laugh; ended in an almost tragic event of not only ending my life but more. All I remember after that was my

Mother taking my hand and placing it in the bathroom sink to run water over it. She and my Dad, who was drunk at the time, rushed me to the emergency room. I remember the bright lights, a cold waiting room and my drunken Father yelling at the hospital staff to hurry up.

Pretty terrifying experience for a young child at the age of 3 don't ya think? The first 10 years of my life consisted of pain, hurt, stress and abandonment. One traumatic event after another was all I had. I wish I could say I have totally healed from most of the experiences in my young childhood, but my destructive teenage years disrupted any sense of healing.

Accept, don't expect!

My Father was a strong man, always worked out lifting weights, was physically active but was known for his temper. He chose to fight a lot while growing up and into his adulthood, especially when he was drunk. After I had turned four years old, my Father had become sick and tired of being sick and tired. He reached out to a co-worker for help about his addiction to alcohol and how his life had become unmanageable. He found a 12 step recovery program that not only saved his life but changed the way he parented also. I had a choice; I could be angry at my Father and chose to look at all the negative he had done. Or I could accept that he had changed.

I learned through years of counseling and 12 step recovery programs, I didn't cause his addiction. I can't control it and I can't cure him. What a relief! I can only have control over myself and my actions.

Today, my Dad is one of my best friends. He is always there for me, just a phone call away. He expresses his love for me in a healthy way and continues to grow spiritually and emotionally even as an adult. He celebrated 36 years of sobriety in January 2015. I am so proud of him.

I learned to accept others instead of expecting them to be perfect. My parents did the best they could with what they had as a young couple.

Today, I have no anger or resentment toward my parents. I focus on the people that love me, like my parents, and spend my energy on them. Life is too short to not love the ones that love me.

3 choices with 3 pieces!

Hustling is learned at an early age. Some adults call it 'manipulative' or 'just being bad.' When you grow up wanting something so badly but the money is not there to buy it, you get creative. No, I am not talking about stealing!

I do, however, have a funny story about stealing though. I was in fifth grade (many years ago!) and my parents let me go to the county fair (small town fun right?) with a friend. Between all those crazy rides and greasy foods, too bad they didn't have fried candy bars back then; my friend and I took a break and walked up to some vendor tables where a woman was selling shell rings. I took one ring out of the velvety display box in an attempt to try it on. With my chunky knuckles and man hands, I forced the shell ring onto my right middle finger.

Unfortunately, the ring got stuck! In an eager desperation to remove it quickly, I grabbed the ring with my left hand, gripped it as tightly as I could and yanked. The beautiful shell ring went flying through that crisp, cool fall air about 10 feet, fell to the hard, concrete floor and broke into 3 pieces!

I had 3 choices at that moment:

#1 Tell the seller at the table what happened, apologize and hand her the 3 broken pieces of the ring and pay the consequence.

#2 Run away.

#3 Pick up the pieces and run away!

I chose to pick up the 3 broken pieces of this beautiful shell ring and run away. As my heart was pounding incredibly hard, the guilt flooded over me like cold water from an ocean wave.

How could I just steal this item? Now I can be arrested. Now I have to live with this decision. How could I be so stupid?

My friend and I left the fair. I walked into my house with a face of shame, frustration and disappointment. I remember my Mom, who is the sweetest woman I have ever met, asking me if I had fun at the fair.

I thought to myself…*FUN? Is becoming a criminal FUN? I stole something! I should turn myself into the police and find a one piece orange jump suit that fits me since I will be going to jail forever! I'm gonna be the next big idiots on one of those cops shows! They should change the words to "Bad girl, bad girl whatcha gonna do, whatcha gonna do when they come for you?"*

But instead, I looked at my Mom, reached into my back pocket of my no name tight jeans and pulled out the 3 broken pieces of that beautiful shell ring. A single tear started the Niagara Falls of sobbing as I confessed to my Mother that I stole the ring after it shattered into pieces.

My Mom picked up the 3 broken pieces out of my hand and encouraged me to stop crying. She looked intently at the 3 pieces of that beautiful shell ring and as she walked away said, "Don't worry honey; some glue will fix this right up!"

WHAT? I thought to myself! *I just stole something from a fair and you just want to fix it so I can wear it?* Like I said, my Mom is the sweetest woman and instead of making me feel worse then I already did, she wanted to 'fix' the problem.

I took that ring after she had glued it together and threw it away in the garbage. The lesson I learned was that I will work hard for everything I get in life. I will never steal anything ever again!

I became a hustler; I worked hard creating ways to make money to purchase anything I wanted. My sister and I created a putt putt golf course in our huge corner lot yard. We borrowed our Dad's putter and golf balls, buried a cup and set up some bricks to create an obstacle course for the neighbors to entertain themselves during the summer. We charged money for each 'hole' and made quite a bit of fun spending money.

We also invested some money into fabric from the corner store. I created 'bathing suits' with the fabric and yarn. Not sure how they held up in the water, but they were cute!

Till this day, my sister and I use our entrepreneur skills in running our own businesses. My sister is brilliant and one of the most talented and hardest working individuals I know.

What the what?

As a rebellious, very active (yes, I was extremely hyper) nine year old, I begged my parents to allow me to ride my bike a few miles away to my friend's house to play football. Oh yeah, I was totally a 'Tom Boy' that loved playing football!

The ride consisted of a few hills, a busy shopping center parking lot and a major road to cross, then smooth sailing on a straight sidewalk to my friend's house. My Mother instructed me to stay on the sidewalk, look both ways and never ride on the 'busy' roads. Oh yeah, and one more important suggestion, ride around the shopping center on the sidewalk, do not ride through the parking lot.

As I jumped on my long, bright yellow, banana looking bike seat that had huge colorful daisies on it; you know I did not pick that thing out! If it was up to me, I would have had a camouflage boys bike; sturdy and fast!

The handle bars were huge and reminded me of bull horns, they started low and raised up so high I could literally straighten my arms in front of me and grab hold of the handles. I loved this bike, the shape, but not the colors!

I took off, huffin'-n-puffin' to pedal myself to the top of the first hill, beside my house. I made it, task one…completed.

Now I was approaching the 'busy' road my Mother warned me about. I steadied myself on my bright yellow 70's style bike and remembered to look both ways as I crossed the street safely. I began my ride around the shopping center parking lot on the sidewalk, remember Mom said, *"Do not ride through the parking lot Tina."*

Yes! I was so proud of myself that I actually listened and followed directions! I made it to the other side of the parking lot and had to cross the 'busy' road for the last leg to my friend's house. The excitement began and questions whipped throughout my brain. *Which position will you be playing in this football game Tina? Are you going to get a touchdown Tina?* I was pumping myself up to get ready for the major game of all football games in the neighborhood.

I made it to my friend's house and we had the best football games ever. I scored numerous touchdowns and knew it was time for this famous footballer to head back home. After playing so much, my legs were a little sluggish; however, I did remember what my Mom instructed, *'to ride on the sidewalk around the shopping center.'*

So, I followed her instructions, rode my bike

around the sidewalk and came to one of the entrances to the parking lot from the 'busy' road. I did not remember all the traffic earlier when I passed this entrance before, so I slowed down to a stop, placed my feet on the ground and waited for the cars to enter and exit the parking lot.

One car stopped, they were smiling at me as if to congratulate me on my hard work of riding my bike by myself to my friend's house and obeying what my Mom instructed. I stood proudly and patiently waiting for all the cars to enter and exit the parking lot. That stopped car waved me on to cross in front of them. I thought to myself, *'how nice!'* I placed my right foot up on my right pedal, and just before taking off to cross, I glanced behind me to be sure no cars were coming behind me to enter the parking lot.

As I placed my left foot up on the left pedal

and my body rose to put pressure on each foot to quickly move me forward to cross; I heard something, something someone on a bike never wants to hear. I heard tires screech and the next thing I know, BAMMMMM! I was hit!

A huge SUV came quickly into the parking lot from a drive way across the street. As I lay on top of the hood of the SUV, my first thought was *MY bikeeeee! Where was my bike?* My second thought was *those stupid people waved me on and caused this accident!*

As I slid off the hood of the SUV, I felt anger in me that I never felt before. The damage was real; my chain fell off my bright yellow bike and I had 2 flat tires from the impact of crashing into the front left tire of the SUV. My long, cool handle bars were scratched, dented and misshapen. But, the worse of all, no one came out of their cars to check to see if I was okay. No one called the police or paramedics.

I grabbed my scuffed up, dented, broken bike and as I tried to walk with it, I realized a cold liquid rushing down my leg, it was the blood gushing from my knees down onto my tennis shoes. My anger quickly turned to rage. I thought to myself, *Why did I trust that driver that waved me on? Why was that SUV speeding? Why doesn't anyone care that I just got hurt?*

I hobbled my broken bike all the way home, and yes, I walked it around the shopping center on the sidewalk, which was safer! (Insert sarcasm.)

It was a long, painful walk home, humbling and scary. The lesson I learned was that I can live with anger and rage and probably hurt myself or others or I can recycle my pain into motivation to change my attitude. I did everything right, followed instructions, followed the law and was super cautious and I still got injured and had consequences.

Pain has value if you use it positively to affect you and your life. Anger is a feeling that hides many feelings below it like sadness, hurt and jealousy. When I can identify that I am feeling angry, I need to ask myself *why* and transform that into a motivator to change me. Pain can motivate me positively.

What's your brand?

Like many young people, I wanted to fit in. I thought if I had the same name brand clothing as them or the most popular brands, they would like me. I would fit in and be valued by what I wore.

Nothing is further from the truth. What a waste of time and energy! First of all, when we rely on what we wear or what car we drive, we are begging for others to 'accept' us and placing their opinion of us above our own. The best lesson I learned in speaking in front of thousands and performing comedy is that if I do not accept and appreciate myself first, no one will accept or appreciate me. Some clothing is nice and some cars are nicer than others but I like to keep it simple. Does it cover me up? Then the clothing is doing its job. Does the car transport me from one place to another? Then the car is doing its job.

It was at this same age, I realized that I value my family. My Father is blind in one eye because he sacrificed his life for all of us living in America by serving in the Army and fighting in the Vietnam War. In eighth grade, we had a choir concert and my parents came to listen to me perform. They are my number 1 fans by the way and attended every game, concert and school function.

The next day in school, a tall boy looked at me and made fun of my Dad's eye, the eye he sacrificed to save this boy's life! The eye that he is blind in because he chose to volunteer for the war at 18 years old.

I typically did not have a temper but that is my DAD and how dare you make fun of him. I grabbed the tall boy's shirt, gathered it up in my right hand and pushed him up against the wall as if I was jacking him up to blast him in the face with the biggest punch I had in me. I stood at barely five feet tall but there was a power behind my anger that I felt superhero strength. I bet I could have thrown him out a window.

I looked the boy in the eyes and said, "Don't you EVER, EVER make fun of my Dad EVER again!"

I will never forget that day in English class; the dark wood floors, the radiator heaters along the windows and the distinguishing moment when I, Tina, stood my ground to one of the tallest boys with the biggest mouths in my class; the school bully!

I learned at an early age, if you dress a pig up in a tuxedo, it is still a pig. In other words, if I lost everything: all of my clothes, all of my belongings, purses, cars, toys or electronics…would I still be Tina? Would I still be valuable? The answer is simply…Yes.

But, my word of advice…do not EVER make fun of my family! Who's with me?

Who am I?

As the youngest in a family of two children, I had a sister that was 4 years older than me. She was great at everything! Do you have a sibling like that? Very outgoing, organized, beautiful and talented…these are only a few characteristics to describe her.

While growing up, my sister was like my Lil' Mama. She taught and helped me with everything; meals, laundry, walking me to school, taking me to my class, playing with me and most of all being an incredible best friend. Everyone should have a sister like mine.

All the positives were outweighed by a huge negative though for a young girl growing up with such an incredible older sibling. Everyone would call me *Michelle's little sister*.

This devastated me as a teenager in junior high school. Being 4 years apart, most of her teachers were my teachers. Their expectations of me were the same expectations they had for my sister. Clearly these professionals did not get the memo that even though we may share the same last name and look alike, we are VERY different!

I struggled for many years living in the shadow of my sister. No fault of my sister at all. One day, my Dad in a heartfelt conversation advised me to just be me. *Make a name for yourself, Tina.* He knew too well the struggle I was having since he had 2 older brothers of his own.

With a mission from my Father, I was going to be me! I started participating in sports; sports that my sister did not participate in like tennis. I hung out with everyone at school, gained respect from many and even though my sister and I shared the same love of theatre and speech, we did share the same love for those 'comedic' roles.

If you are feeling lost or in the shadow of your older sibling or maybe a sibling or a relative that is in the spotlight, please remember you just need to be you. Each of us have our own special talents and gifts. What are yours? How can you share a piece of you with the world to make an identity for yourself?

That's not love!

As a teenager, you start to notice one another and may become attracted to each other. I noticed a boy, who was a little older than me and he told me all the right things I never heard before. "You are so pretty! I LOVE you! I can't live without you!"

As an impressionable young lady, trying to find my own identity; I fell victim to all of the 'words' this boy desperately repeated to me. Soon after the start of the relationship, he requested some private one on one time alone with me and isolated me from everyone else. He took me to a place that not even my loudest scream could be heard and he violated me. He hurt me, not just with his 'words' but his actions this time. The abuse lasted for one year.

For many years, I told myself I deserved it. I

was not worthy of anyone else. I thought I needed a controlling boy in my life to tell me what to do and how to do it. I transformed into a helpless victim that was at the beckon call of an abuser, a rapist and a manipulator. It was not just him that distorted my relationships in high school, it was the 'cookie cutter' boys that followed in his footsteps that I allowed to destroy me slowly, one agonizing ugly word at a time, one punishing physical punch at a time and one violating sexual action at a time which continued into later years with one gun pointed at my head and the trigger was pulled by a so-called boyfriend. My spirit was stolen and the hurt brewed beneath my skin as my heart was surrounded by a stone cold wall to protect it.

It was not until college, when I overheard my roommates sharing their fairy tale experiences with their first boyfriends that I realized my relationships were not even close to the fairy tales I dreamt of while growing up. I learned that I suffered for many years from domestic violence, rape and abuse. I realize now that No means No! Respect it and respect me.

If you are in a relationship or can relate to my past, please tell someone and ask for help. There are many resources available to help you. Never settle for someone that does not respect you, or for someone who does not love you for you or someone who does not cherish your every word or action. You are worthy of true love, a love that does not hurt.

One of the things that saved my life was journaling. I love to write, well of course, you are reading one of my books! I had to separate my negative feelings on paper and make a gratitude list to convince myself that there were positive aspects to my life. It was not all doom and gloom. There is always help and someone that has gone through what you have gone through. A support group can help and so does counseling. Share your secrets. When you bring light to darkness, you will start to heal. In order to heal, you have to feel.

You are enough!

Even though my relationships left me battered, heartbroken and abused; my tiny spirit still miraculously lived on. Actually, I gained more courage and faith afterwards than ever before. Is there anything that makes you feel like you are not enough?

Are you proud of your weight? Are you comfortable in your own skin?

As a past gymnast, cheerleader, tennis player, softball player and track sprinter, I constantly worried about my appearance and weight. I remember never enjoying getting weighed, still till this day I hate going to the doctors and being weighed before they even ask how I am doing. I always ask the nurse to jump up on those scales first before me so I can make her feel ashamed of eating that huge hot fudge brownie sundae for breakfast! Okay, maybe not for breakfast, but probably the night before.

Instead of dreading that walk to the scales and hating the hike atop to capture those miserable, overpowering numbers…write **You are enough** on your scales. I refuse to have numbers dictate my life. Unless of course, I am faced with the question: 'Would you like 2 scoops of ice cream or 3?'

Did you know that you were made on purpose and that every part of your body has a reason it was made that way? I never understood this. And questioned why I was literally created with broad 'man' shoulders. Yes, the kind every adolescent male dreams to have! Not cool when you are a chick! Or is it?

Are you a swimmer? Do you do gymnastics? Wow, look at those shoulders!

These are a few comments I heard over the years. Talk about making you feel self-conscious. I would make sure all of my clothing accentuated a v-neck to distract from these huge broad shoulders.

During the winter, I lived in northern Ohio in my twenties, and on one chilly afternoon, my boyfriend asked me to take a trip into a State Park and go sled riding with him. I agreed to go and that it would be so much fun. He gathered up his young daughter and pregnant sister and off we went. When we got there, my boyfriend made a fire in one of the big metal trash cans at the bottom of what he called "Killer Mountain!" Of course, being the athletic one of the group, I raced up to the top of the snow covered steep hill. His pregnant sister and young daughter met me up there a few minutes later and I insisted that I would 'try out' "Killer Mountain" first.

I jumped onto my sled with so much excitement that it took off from under me, struggling to stay on it; I was off howling over the ice covered snow and whipping by my boyfriend, who stood near the bottom of the hill by the hot fire in the can.

The last thing I remember seeing was a huge ramp in front of me at the bottom of the hill. Snowboarders had built a 4 foot ramp at the bottom of "Killer Mountain" and I was about to take flight.

I held onto the flimsy tiny sled with both of my frozen hands and clenched my teeth in fear for what was about to happen. The paramedics estimated I was traveling at 30 mph and had gone airborne at least 6 feet before landing on my head.

The next thing I knew, the ambulance lights and sirens woke me up as the paramedics were cutting my new down feathered, expensive winter coat and removed my clothing. YES, in the freezing cold, in front of these strangers, I wore nothing but tears and my ugly underwear.

In the hospital, after numerous tests and examinations, the doctors determined that my BIG, muscular broad shoulders saved my life. I had no broken neck, back or bones. The moral of the story, wear cute clean underwear before sled riding! LOL

No, the moral of the story is that every part of your body was created for a purpose and reason.

You are enough!

Seriously?

At a young age, I started disrespecting my body, I used chemicals to try to relax, chill out from stress and escape from hurt and anger. As I grew up and realized that smoking a cigarette, drinking alcohol or smoking marijuana only numbed me for a short period of time, the high never lasted and actually hurt me more than helped. I decided at the age of 23, that drugs and alcohol were not helping me in my life.

For over 17 years, I have worked with youth that have been abused, neglected, drug addicted and criminals. I ask every single one of them the same question: "Will this decision hurt you, help you or heal you?"

When you are about to make a choice that will affect you and your life, because let's be honest, everything you do to your brain, body and heart will affect you for the rest of your life. Don't believe me? Just ask my friend who is paralyzed from the neck down because he made one decision at 16 years old that affected him for the rest of his life. He was drunk and dove into a shallow pool, broke his neck and almost died.

Or my friend that got into a drunken fight at 17 years old and ended up in prison for seven and a half years because he put a dude in a coma.

Have you made some negative choices that could be affecting you and your life? Then ask yourself: Does this hurt me? Does this help me? Does this heal me?

Everything in life ends up in one of these 3 categories. Everything we eat, drink, inhale, inject, swallow or do ends up in one of these 3 categories: Hurt, help or heal. And if you think everything is helping you, then ask those around you if it is really helping. One of the best things my Dad used to say to me while I was growing up, "You are who you hang around with!"

Every time I met a young person that committed a crime or was caught with drugs, I asked them to tell me about their friends, who they hang around with. If they say, well my friends are in jail, or they have a juvenile record, that child's risk factor of being in prison just increased dramatically. I love the quote, "Show me your friends and I will show you your future."

Who we hang around with determines our future. Surround yourself with people that are doing what you want your future to look like.

Am I saying to never try to help others in need? No, I truly believe we can be a light in other people's darkness; however, I do not put myself at risk of danger by doing it. The truth is if nothing changes, nothing changes. People have to want to change. Focus on the people around you that love you and respect you. Do not waste time on your haters, they have nothing to lose. You have everything to lose.

Here's the Homecoming Queen! Oh wait, her crown doesn't fit!

It was my senior year and the Homecoming Dance was approaching quickly. Amongst the mist of the hurriedness of finding a date, a dress to make it a memorable experience, I never in a million years imagined I would have to shop for an outfit to wear to the football Homecoming game.

I was raised to always treat others the way you want to be treated. Well, I actually treated others way better than I ever treated myself but anyways, I did live by that to the best of my abilities. I loved everyone and always tried to make them laugh or feel better than I first met them. Y.O.L.O. right? You only live once so make a respectful name for yourself.

The voting began for the Homecoming court. To be honest, I did nothing or said nothing to even remotely consider myself as a contender. I was friends with so many incredible young ladies that deserved to reign as the queen. They worked very hard, got awesome grades and were really 'good' girls.

I, on the other hand, became a raging alcoholic that got barely passing grades, was extremely selfish, boy crazy and had no hope for my future. If that was my biography beside my name on the voter ballet, do you think anyone would have voted for me?

The announcement came over the loud speaker, I was joking around with someone in class and the kid stopped and asked, "Don't you want to hear this?"

I dismissed it without any hope that I would hear the syllables of my name come across that sound system to announce the

Homecoming Court for our class of 1993. Friend's names were heard one by one and the anticipation was not felt by me but many of my classmates that wanted to see me be voted.

Surprisingly, I had made the top 5 for Homecoming court. *WHAT?* I thought to myself. How the heck did that happen?

The big night came and I agreed to wear a nice, professional suit with a scarf in hopes that the restaurant we would receive a free dinner at would mistakenly think I was over 21 years old and serve me alcohol. Really? I am a senior in high school at the Homecoming Football Game and I have a suit on? It was nice and I did get some use out of it in the future for a few interviews.

My escort stood with his arm linked beneath mine and we stood there in the crisp cold evening along with the 4 other young beautiful ladies and their escorts. The announcer introduced us and thank God my Dad videotaped it because I literally fell into a trance by what someone said to me seconds before my name was announced over the sound system. He said, "Don't get upset Tina, but you didn't get Homecoming Queen!"

After a brief pause, the announcer excitedly yelled, "Tina Miller!" I literally looked at my escort and realized that that was MY name! THAT was my name! That WAS my name called out in front of thousands of people! And with a shuffle of our feet, my escort walked me to the thrown where I was crowned the Homecoming Queen by one of my best friends, Deidra (Homecoming Queen, class of 1992).

Wait a minute, that crown does not fit me! I am too little, too weak, too shallow, too messed up to ever fit in something so beautiful, prestigious, honoring and shiny. My self worth was about the size of a mustard seed and there was no telling when that crown was going to crash to the fake football field grass beneath me. I looked at my parents, both of which were standing there crying while videoing me the whole time.

If actually being crowned Homecoming Queen was not enough, I had a huge picture centerfold in our year book and everyone knew me as the Queen, class of 1993.

An honor yet curse, a dream yet nightmare, how will I ever tell others of my character defects, lying, and manipulative, drunken behaviors without having this crown taken away? What if they knew the real me?

I felt that curse for many years, until I shared my story of overcoming abuse, addictions and adversities and realized that many other people have been through all the troubles I had been through and the difference is I made it out alive, healthy and willing to help others.

Today, I may not wear a Homecoming Queen crown or sit on a thrown, but I feel like a queen. No, not a drama queen or a rich person living in a palace married to a king. Today, I base my feelings on my faith and know deep down inside, I am treasured, I am worthy and I am loved by my Creator.

True Value…it's not just a store!

Have you ever realized how many numbers there are everyday that can represent you? If you get a cup of coffee, you receive a receipt with 'your number' on it. When you are in school, you get a 'student ID number.' When you are born in the United States of America, you get issued a 'social security number' that identifies you for the rest of your life. When you get in the deli line at the grocery store to order lunch meat, you have to get a number.

I know I promised we were not going to do any Math since the first chapter; I will keep to my promise. No Math.

Recently in the tall building, where my office is located in downtown Tampa I was headed onto the elevator. It is a very busy building with every adult and juvenile that is on probation or parole visiting their assigned officer that supervises their probation or parole period in county. I was standing in the elevator and overheard an adult man say to a young man while pointing to his Department of Corrections identification card and said, "This right here is my number, I will never forget my number for the rest of my life." It was his DOC# that the state prison gave him when he got arrested for committing a crime or crimes.

This short interaction with this man made me feel so sad for him and many others that end up in the system; they believe they are only a number.

I want to encourage you as a young person, do not just become a number. You are valuable; you are not just another number. If you have a number, bring life and positive choices to that number. Make that number valuable because you are MORE valuable than any ole' number.

You are responsible for you and your actions. If you have stress or pressures in life, you can allow it to define you, destroy you or strengthen you. Those numbers can define you. It is your choice to let it destroy you. I have witnessed many people get rehabilitated and recover from a past of crime and addictions; however, I have seen more people let it destroy them, their families and friends.

Remember your true value.

But, she was so happy!

Ever feel so down you just cannot find a solution? Feel like the world is crashing around you and you just want it to stop? Have you ever thought if it all just ended now, you would feel so much better?

These are all questions I am sure she answered 'yes!' too.

She is my friend that I met in a 12 step recovery program that had a smile that lit up a room when she walked in. Her warm hugs were enough to say to you *'it's going to be okay.'*

Then one day, she was not there. I never saw her smile again. I never felt her warm hug again. I never got that call that asked how I was doing again. And I never got to say good bye. My friend committed suicide.

Now I understand the signs of suicidal people

and unfortunately, have experienced numerous friends commit suicide, the signs are about as clear as mud. How can someone I just saw smiling, happy and full of joy shoot themselves in their head the next day? How can a friend not call me one last time to say I am not feeling right can you talk?

I will never forget the day I found out she killed herself. We had planned a weekend camping, boating and fishing together in her trailer at the lake. She had bright future plans and was looking forward to a relaxing time with me. A couple of days before the trip, I received a call from a mutual friend that informed me that our friend was no longer alive. There would be no trip, no laughs, no camping, no time well spent together ever again.

As I was driving down the highway on a beautiful blue sky day, I punched my steering wheel in a fit of rage, screaming out "How could you do this? How could you leave me? How could you just ruin everything?" I felt so much anger toward my friend. How dare her kill herself! How selfish!

Over the years, I learned about mental health and how important it is to keep communicating with friends and loved ones that are suicidal. And if I witness them extremely happy about life, on one of their 'highs', or in one of those extremely 'low' times, I need to ask them if they are planning on harming themselves. Other signs I missed were the 'final plans' she had been preparing for the last few weeks. She was organizing her finances, signing over bank accounts to her husband, canceling contracts and writing good bye letters.

As much as I want to take responsibility for everyone and try to save everyone, I cannot.

It was not my fault. I did everything I could to show her I loved her. I must detach with love even if it hurts to think about the times we had together. The anger, hurt and sadness motivates me today to help others.

If you know of someone that is talking about suicide, obsessed with death or giving away valuables, please talk with them and get them help. At the back of this book, I have provided resources (websites and phone numbers). Please use them. No one deserves to live a death sentence. No temporary problem deserves a permanent conclusion. I miss my friends that committed suicide. To honor them and their lives, I will help myself and others to prevent anyone else from feeling that loss.

Just for today.

Tomorrow is not here yet. Today is a gift and yesterday is over. *Just for today*, focus on what YOU have control over. Take it one minute at a time if you have to. Prioritize your tasks by saying, 'first things first'. What has to be done right now? What can wait?

Life is precious. As I write this, I just found out another young life was taken too soon. A young boy was accidentally killed. I met with him and his Mom just 3 weeks ago. The last thing I suggested to him was "Do not hang with the boys that are not going where you want to go in your future." In other words, stop running away, disobeying your Mom and realize these boys that encourage that behavior are not your 'friends'.

Guess who shot him, those supposedly 'friends.' I feel so sad that his Mother has to bury him. She will not be picking out his 8th grade graduation suit, but picking out his suit to be buried in. If you have lost a friend through a tragic accident or crime, you know the anger and hurt.

After 33 years of losing my friend in 2nd grade, I still wonder if she would have gotten married or had children. What she would be like as an adult? There is a piece of my 7 year old heart that was laid to rest the day of her funeral. I had to learn that it was not my fault she was kidnapped and murdered.

If you have ever lost a loved one, please talk with someone about the sadness, grief, hurt and pain you may feel. Until I did that, I carried 'survivor guilt' which is always feeling guilty that I survived and that she did not. You are alive for a reason.

Find your purpose and live your passion.

Just for now, I am saying good bye. My hope is that you gained a 'little' inspiration and a 'little' motivation from this 'little' book with BIG truth. I hope to see you at your school or in your community soon. If you want to hear me speak, please check out my website at www.tinatalkstruth.com and contact me.

I would love to hear from you. You can call, email or just follow me on social media. I want to remind you of a few 'little' reminders I hope you take with you each day.

Oh yeah, I almost forgot to share with you the BIG T.R.U.T.H. that I share with many teens your age:

T.=Talk…are you talking the talk but not walking the talk? So many times I hear teens say something then watch them act out the opposite way. Don't waste your time and energy trying to 'talk the talk' then not walking that talk. In other words, actions speak louder than your words. People will watch you more than listen to you.

R.=Real? Are you being real with you? As adolescents, it can be easy to just do what you think everyone else is doing. What do you want to do? How do you want others to think of you? What do you want others to say about you? Be yourself and be real!

U.=Understand, do you try to understand others? Not everyone grew up like you in the same neighborhood, with the same family or felt like you as a child. Try to keep an open mind. People act a certain way because they are reacting to their circumstances. Try to understand why they are so miserable before judging them.

T.=Trust, if you can't trust yourself, how will others trust you? Seriously, no one is perfect! Forgive yourself for your mistakes and start a fresh new life today. When you make a mistake or say something hurtful to someone, accept responsibility and apologize then move on.

H.=Hurt, help, or heal? Ask yourself before making a decision: Will this hurt me? Help me? Or heal me? If it will hurt you, don't do it! If it will help or heal you, then do it! And by help, I mean, will this help you succeed in life? Not just help relieve stress temporarily.

That's the BIG T.R.U.T.H. in this book! These are the helpful tactics and the results of working with young people for over 17 years in the fields of social work, drug treatment/prevention and juvenile justice. Honesty, integrity, loyalty and responsibility are so important as you grow up.

8 simple things you learned in this book:

1. You have a purpose…find it.

2. Stop hiding…and "B true 2 U!" No one else can be you…you are unique!

3. Keep an open mind, not everyone has your life.

4. Stop people pleasing.

5. You can only control you & your actions.

6. Use anger as a motivator to make a positive change.

7. Ask yourself: will this hurt me? Help me? Or heal me?

8. Remember your true value.

TTYL

I am horrible with endings, so here's one last thing. I expect you to have fun and just do you. Just B U!

My dream for you is to find peace within you; respect yourself, chose positive people to encourage you and love you for you, and last but not least, ask for help if you ever feel like the pressure is too much to live your life.

Live a life sentence today, not a death sentence due to the pressure of things.

RESOURCES

According to the National Suicide Prevention Lifeline:

Suicide is the 3rd leading cause of death for teens.

If you feel like you want to hurt yourself, please call 1-800-273-8255.

www.suicidepreventionlifeline.org

Why do some drug users become addicted?

- Family History
- Abuse, neglect or other traumatic experiences in childhood
- Mental disorders
- Early use of drugs
- Method of administration (smoking or injecting may increase potential)

Call 1-800-662-HELP in the U.S. if you need help and support for drug abuse.

www.helpguide.org

Women ages 16-24 experience the highest per capita rates of intimate violence.
(US Department of Justice, 1997)

1 in every 4 women will experience domestic violence in her lifetime. www.safehorizon.org

On average, 24 people per minute are victims of rape, physical violence or stalking by an intimate partner in the United States – more than 12 million women and men over the course of a year.
www.cdc.gov/violenceprevention

Are you being abused or neglected?
Please call 1-800-422-4453.
www.teenshealth.org

As a recovering alcoholic, drug addict, recovery advocate and abuse and rape survivor, I feel it is extremely important to offer these resources to help you. If you do not want to call or check out the websites, please talk to someone you trust. Someone cares about you. And if you still cannot find someone, please email me at

tinatalkstruth@gmail.com

I care!

You matter to me!

And you <u>DO</u> make a difference. –

Tina

Made in the USA
San Bernardino, CA
17 October 2016